AF479883

SMALL STONES ON TRAILS

SMALL STONES ON TRAILS

Daniel Heagerty

1950-2022

For my beloved children,
Lauren and Casey

Being your father has been the greatest gift of my life.
I know you will be fine when I move on.
Take good care of each other for me.
You always have my love.
These poems are my final gift of love to you.

FOREWARD

Let my vital force now attain the immortal air.
Now let this body be reduced to ashes.
Om, O my mind,
Remember – remember all that has been done.
Remember – remember all that has been done.

– ISA UPANISAD

Daniel was intrigued by the contemplation of nature in poetry. In poems written in the T'ang and Sung dynasties, he found a way to satisfy his hankering for a world outside his four walls. He found spirituality and humor. He found a window to view mankind in terms of our universe, finding wisdom.

Daniel thrived in images of the journey. River crossings on small boats with bamboo poles and lanterns; Cold Mountain, gushing streams and mist, whispering pines, cups of wine, contemplation of the world. In time, these images grew second nature to him, always in mind; bringing reflection and laughter to his life and his poems.

Reflecting on family, friends, nature, joy, failure, with an eye to the meaning of it all, Daniel scribed poems forming a trail of his life. His heart, intention and compassion are shared herein. As Daniel loved to quote the Sung dynasty poet Su Tung-P'O, "Victory is hopeless. Truce will have to do."

His spirit is immortal, and in these poems, Daniel lives.

– NED HEAGERTY

PROLOGUE: A PRESCIENT POEM

The Longer I Live
March 23, 1996

The longer I live
The more experiences I have
The less fear I have of death
The less anxiety of its absoluteness
The less attached to what may be missed.

TABLE OF CONTENTS

POEMS FOR A DRIFTING PLANET
January 3, 1997

A festival of poets
Each sitting alone, spread across continents
Mountain ridges, river shores, creek edges
Poems for a drifting planet
In a universe of universes
To mark the 9th Day of the 9th Month
For thirteen centuries
Contemplating
Poems scribed, poems emerging
Alone only in time.

IN THE DISTANCE

An old tilted porch, peeling paint
City lights veiled behind tall firs.

A settling, into the waning summer
Contemplating fall colors of maple, cottonwood
Heavy rains and falling leaves.

Reflecting on our distance,
What we share, on this day, a thousand miles apart
You, like me, caught in the space of lines of a poem.

The art of living, not so easy,
Poetry we use to record and disclose
Passed paths, their patterns and switchbacks.

Seeking words that might capture fleeting insights
Not so easy, images pass through time
Like wind passing through grass.

Another year of poems
Another year of leaves grown, then dropped

Too many words now past, like the morning's mist.

DRYING THE INK

1993

The day a grinding struggle
Demands and distractions relentless
The sun lost, as fatigue greets nightfall
Paths of life usually quiet, but today busy with restless
    activity,
demands of those not settled
Each acknowledgment conjures a poem seeking ink
For this 9th Day of the 9th Month.

Another season poised to pass
Birds gather to fatten for fall flights.

I struggle to find the right setting
Searching for tendrils to connect me to my brother
I wander home from the day's din
Descend to the creek's soft, quiet edge
Settle amongst the tall grasses
And breathe the silken breeze of late summer.

Coming into the quietness
A smile emerges that extends to the moon
Knowing my brother is also scratching at paper

Drying his ink beside a different stream
One thousand miles south
Honoring the great Taoist poets.

9TH DAY OF THE 9TH MONTH

2005

To the great poets
Of the Sung and T'ang Dynasties
I bow with praise

To two poets I know
Who today will scribe their poems in the same honor
I send gratitude.

Aware of both discord and harmony
Neither short or quick
But that urge to push for verse more complex, richer

The air in the Garden smells of early fall
And the dispatch of another season in transformation
To end, and build, on the summer's growth.

SEPTEMBER'S COTTONWOODS

Late summer red sun pulls orange and yellow from the over-
    story
Draws a deep blue from the passing river

Soothing scents of pine and sage ride the soft breeze
On this 9th Day of the 9th Month

Cottonwoods thick in golden leaf
Full in cottonseed hulls, ready to float the river

Once again, time to harvest poems
For winter nights by the fire.

RAIN-SMEARED POEMS

1992

I

Night warm and dark,
Moon barely illuminates the page
Beneath the pines
Reflections on past years of the 9th Day
With my brother, scratching out poems in honor of the
    T'ang poets.

Once, on the shores of Puget Sound
Ducking under low-stooped spruce
We laughed at relentless rain squalls
Trading pen and paper back and forth
Building on each other's lines
And careless with the wine
Careless with the gods.
Where rest those rain-smeared poems
From so many years ago?

II

I think of all our years
Traveling into the high country, for this day
Immersing our heads in ice-melt streams

Thrusting ourselves across rolling landscapes of imagination.
I see you
As a silhouette in the gold-magenta sunset
Filling the desert expanse
Knowing our poems will fall short of our hopes.

The popping of the campfire
The creaking of field chairs as we dodge resin-rich smoke
Dreams curl like flames through our conversations
As you read poems of the masters of the Sung and T'ang
    Dynasties
Their verses of rivers and mountains, without end.

I start another poem
We argue spatial dimensions,
Agree on avenues to harmony
Seeking the unanticipated, challenging boundaries
Always content, at the end of the 9th Day.

POEM TO THE T'ANG POETS
2015

I

The clear pools of the Yuba River, that inescapable invitation
Granite slabs warmed even with a low sun
Water cold in the early autumn air
The body chills quick, to the spine
Then warmed by the granite block against bare skin
Once again, lulled to sleep at the river's edge
To be lost in dreams of a past never to be again.

II

No moon to rise this 9th Day of 9th Month
The sky ink black but for a billion stars
The galaxy a shining veil from ridgetop to ridgetop
Sparkling in the high Sierra crispness

III

Moonless, the sky commands an unhampered glow
The depths of the galaxy profoundly evident
Light traversing distances beyond comprehension
Shimmering and outside of time
A map of unlimited possibilities, beyond imagination.

IV

No sounds but for water passing through boulder blocks
The star densities emulate patterns of cirrus clouds
Is it night or is it day, is there a difference
In all this stillness, a whisper
That anything to ever be created, or ever imagined
At our most inspired, has already eclipsed.

V

If we transcend, to see the not so obvious
To sense the far greater, glimpse the unexplainable
Consciousness proves unlimited
Yet a view of just this universe
Even a searching imagination for what lies beyond
Renders a consciousness still wanting.

VI

Enamored with discoveries in the material world
Technological advances bent to ease the deep pain of living
While the universe remains untouched, neutral, patient
While we draw low on time, our developing consciousness
    too slow
To meet our reckless burn through earth's habitat
Fooling ourselves because we can.

VII

If only we could rejoin the source of energy
The light of all galaxies
No longer separated by delusions of special or divined
Instead released, set free of separateness
Back into pure light, pure energy
Where lays the Perfect Poem.

9TH DAY OF 9TH MONTH
2018

In last stages of light, the mountain peak in striking
    silhouette
Birds quiet
Coyotes soon to call across the canyon.
Stars in unimpeded symmetry
Constellations filling the blackening sky.

Whatever happened today is done, forever past
Dropping away, as daylight into night
Tomorrow awaits, a cart loaded with unknowns
Only to pass into yet another yesterday, then a distant past
Falling away like stars into the next dawn.

PART TWO
NATURE SHORTS

.

SPEAK

Speak
With the clear, unequivocal lucidity
Of a madman
Free of hypocrisy
No longer to abide by a reality
That makes no sense.

COMPOST

A thousand small invertebrates with every turn of the
   pitchfork
An ecosystem rich in color, vibrant in life
Tomatoes will be deep red, corn stalks over my heart.

MOSS IN THE JAPANESE GARDEN

I

Rays of sunlight
Piercing through tall firs
Stone patterns float in soft moss.

II

Patterns of rake in sand
The Flat Garden dappled by sun
A hundred colors of green moss.

III

Winter's softness
Captured in warm sunlight
Bending caressing moss.

IV

Deep in the darkness of forest
Meager light drawn from lichen and ground-moss
The sky ominous, penetrating.

HAIKUS OF JULY

July 3-4, 2012

I

Bright silver moon
Arcs into the gold of western peaks
The sun crests the east ridge

II

Stillness of the high mountains
In the golden light of dawn
Here, now, to behold and be humbled

III

Facing the east at sunrise
Lost in the Tao
A squirrel scampers over my shoulders

IV

Writing poems
In the warmth of the rising sun
My daughter in sun salutation

V

Grey-blue of distant ridge
Lifts the full moon into the high mountains
Horizon a silhouette of endless pines

VI

Dawn in the high mountains
Both impenetrable and accessible
Each morning a choice

PART THREE

THE ANTHROPOCENE

UNFOLDING BEFORE OUR EYES

Larger than life
Reshaping all life
The pandemic rolls across the globe
Smart, impressive, adaptive, mutating
Feeding on its host, us, and our failed humanity.

As with climate, a preponderance of denials
Realities ignored, narratives conceived for convenience
Political action limited to serve the politicians
While destitution and starvation envelop the 3rd world
Fed by the arrogance of the wealthy.

Property and wealth above community, the commons
A disproportionate harm of ethnic groups, the socially
    disadvantaged
Racism furthered in silent acquiescence
The bible the prop void of the moral compass
Climate inaction, pandemic about me not us.

The failure of humankind
To act as a community, as an interdependent species
To embrace the realities of climate catastrophe, pandemic
    surges

Will be a signature of the Anthropocene
The species that chose self over community and future
    generations.

Atmospheric destruction for industry profits,
The me, not we, response to existential threats
Wall Street gorging on greed
Politicians singularly focused on elections/fundraising
Freedom defined by self-interest.

Viruses flourish, the planet cascades to overheating
As we give witness to the gorging profiteers devoid of moral
    compass
In this growing mayhem we record the Anthropocene, the
    human epic
Life in the great collapse, left to our future generations and
    species
An unfathomable shame.

ANTICIPATION OF TOMORROW

Tomorrow to be met with anticipation
Will there be a more perfect setting
Will the air be softer
The thoughts more comforting
The light more soothing
Sounds more gentle
Smells more transformative
Anxieties diminished
Memories freed of discomfort.
Or will tomorrow be like today
Hiding its splendor and perfection
In a distracted mind.

POST JULY 4TH BLUES

The pull of the Sierra Mountains
Grows stronger, more needed
The granite walls now warm, everyday
Summer runoff strong, water also warmer

The smell of Jeffery pines
Calls of the Clark's nutcracker
The lazuli skies unveiled at elevation 8,000 feet
Poems stuffed into pockets

I want out of the city, into the high country
Leave the relentless noise of man and machine
The wasted toil of grooming lawns, blowing fallen leaves
The ceaseless news of greed, hurt, war, injustice and fragility

Again and again, every year, a pattern of failure
How do we abdicate to such distortion and disappointment
In a country supposedly founded on high values, noble
    aspirations
Only to deny our repeated failures of war, selfishness and
    inequality.

PART FOUR

THE TAO OF MY CHILDREN

BIRTHDAY WITH LAUREN

My daughter reads poems from the T'ang Dynasty
Poems of rivers and mountains
As we tuck further into the rock outcropping
With the wind churning up the river
A river now 1,500 miles from its headwaters.
Crows and vultures soar far below
Swallows cluster before their flight through the gorge winds
We sit at cliff's edge and quietly watch
The endless poems unfold, swirl, pass below and above, east
    to west
A most precious gift.

CR GORGE WITH LAUREN - II

Climbing out of the steep gorge of Oneota Creek
Switchbacks reinforced with old basalt stonework.
Saturated soils of winter rains seep water across the trail.
The ridgeline, dry beneath old growth firs
Where we find soft ground to sit, with backs against towering
    trees.
We drink tea, reflect on a companionship
As rich as this glorious setting
Of filtered sunlight caressing the sword fern
And songs of rocky brooks
As solid as the columnar basalt cliffs
Elegant as the floating lichen freed by kinglets overhead.

MOUNT JEFFERSON WILDERNESS WITH CASEY

Two hours of rough trail to mountain lake
The water a glass reflection of Grizzly Peak
We swim to wash off trail dust and sweat
The lake silent but for gray jays, a big horned owl
Once the sun crests the west peaks
We eat a simple dinner, in attentive silence
Alpenglow, gold and pink, softens the rock peaks
And highlights the strips and patches of snow
We whisper of the full moon ascending the east ridge
And direct each other to the emerging glorious cloud
    patterns
The lake turns from blue to silver
Shadow patterns weave through the forest
And we quietly discuss universes beyond ours
Worlds more numerous than man's imagination
Huddled beside a small campfire

WE GLIMPSE THE LUMINOUS MIND. COTTONWOOD BUDS

The warm sun
The soft delicate greens of Indian plum
Precursors for the emerging spring
An effervescence, clear light, the waning of winter.
We walk the pastures and forest
Naming rivers and mountains to visit in summer
We collect bud-laden twigs of the cottonwood
To bring home and watch flower
Filling rooms with sweet smells and inspiration for uncharted
    trails.

AT FOUR YEARS OLD *

Hiraniwa, the Flat Garden,
Pushing out from a perfectly round island of green moss
A pattern of white soft ripples of carefully raked course sand
Bordered by flawless edges of dark stone
Instilling both contemplation and release.

We sit quietly, observing.
I whisper: "The sand is raked daily, for visitors like us
But notice there are no footprints."
You reply, perfectly:
"Maybe the Gardner wears boots
That don't have footprints."

Smiling with that thought
We gaze at the intricate sand ridges
Rippling across the garden
Left by a Master with only a simple wood-toothed rake
Who knows the expanse of no trace
The essence of the unseen.

* Lauren at four

POND BY CABIN

Thirty years ago
We swam to the small rock island
Clinging tightly to my neck, my daughter worried about
     alligators
We talked of habitats, where the different animals live or
     don't live
She relaxed her grip as we approached the island.

On the flat granite rock, leaning over the edge, we looked
     into eight feet of clear water
Imagining and marveling and giggling
Creating a world that makes sense for a three-year-old
Helping her father see the treasures otherwise unseen.

NORTHERN ROCKIES

High in the Northern Rockies
Glaciation dominates the landscape
Lakes emerald and cold
Cirques to the left and right
The rivers run glacial milk.

Son and daughter young, apprehensive, attentive
We scramble up the side of a long waterfall
To a one-room log tea house
Perched on the precipice
The icy air stings our noses.

The old spruce creaks and groans behind us
The view rich, expansive, peaceful
We sip tea quietly
Absorbing the profound landscape of an upturned earth
Overwhelmed by a geology we struggle to imagine.

NESTLED IN BOULDERS

We scrambled up long granite fault blocks
Weathered so boots grip well on steep inclines

At 9,000 feet little hope for warm water
Cold, dive in and scramble out.

We sleep, shoulder to shoulder
On ridgeback, tucked into a boulder swale
Just below summit
My daughter, me, and a million stars.

PART FIVE

NATURE'S SPACES / PLACES

THE GATE TO SEA

I

The horizon, limitless waters of the Pacific
A pure line, slight curvature, slicing sky from sea
Beckoning every thought, each feeling
To open wide the chest and eyes
With no need to be elsewhere.

II

Consciousness relentlessly compromised
Missing the Great Elegance each day, night
Lost in duality, navigating impulses
Missing the interconnectedness of Being
Each day the struggle with self-protection
Not understanding that the singular challenge is not survival
But being inside the splendor of the moment.

III

Rolling in from the vast ocean
Waves of solitary beauty and robustness
Roiling, pushing, caressing rock, sand, cliff
The harmony, the Suchness, only to be missed
By distractions of the more readily identified and described.

IV

Disrespecting and ignoring what nurtures and feeds
The earth's climate now forever altered
Consequences of greed and the choice of ignorance
How great must the willful failures be
The cries of suffering so loud
Before the Earth's wrath overwhelms

V

Decades of my one life spent in disappointment, grief
Witnessing wanton disregard for this planet
A myopic selfish species lost in magical thinking, human
    exceptionalism
Ignoring the breakdown of earth systems, biological
    interdependencies
Moving ever more inescapably to pandemics, famines, fires,
    floods, species demise
Devoid of collective remorse or even honest acknowledgment

VII

Samatha (Pali) opens the door to Perception
The wind seen, heard, smelled, felt, moving through the
    forest
A thousand shades of green
A thousand species in each liter of ocean
Veins, rhizomes, micro cilia marvelously woven in soil
Available, waiting, for the fearless mind.

VIII

Mara, the delusion of life, always the desire for more
Consciousness wrapped in personal wants, veiled in the fear
    of aloneness
Clinging to the fleeting, ethereal senses
Yesterday only as real as the stories conjured
Tomorrow never to manifest as constructed by the mind
A consciousness unable to still the restlessness
The veils obscuring the unfiltered Light.

IX

The ocean, today, as never before
Waves deep, inseparable
A pervasive sensuality, caressing
The dancing of quanta
Streams of blues, greens, golds, silver
Ephemeral veils of light, effervescence, the whirling dervishes
With immeasurable energy
Pulling the mind and soul into deeper water
Sensing the weave of material and non-material
The song of eternity
The code to open the gate.

X

How beautiful, this gift
To see with clarity the One Act benefitting all species, all life
To reunite with the peace of the cosmology
To release all beings otherwise destined to feed one's daily
    demands of living.
End the relentless material demands on earth
The ultimate action, honoring all elements, the Great
    Passage, the Future of Life.

GARDEN STONES

September 13, 2003

Two stones, chest high
Thin, angular, set at the edge of the pavilion
Late afternoon sun caresses one, then the other
Gold stains of ore drip from the dark grey slate
Herbs bask in the stone's reflecting warmth
The cooling air draws a fine mist from old firs
The bamboo sings softly
With the evening thermals.

AUTUMN

September 27, 2008

Morning fog thick, holding a curtain of transition
Days, though still warm, turn into cold nights
Yielding new smells of late season blooms
And stunning oranges and reds of maple trees
Through the sun's shortened arc that sweeps low across the
    earth's crust
Spiders cast their kites of webbing across the trail
Some to capture the last of the winged hatches
Others migrating to new habitats, to lay eggs and die.

Spring births, and new growth, more than just my
    imagination
Living and dying dependent on each other
A truth to hold honorably and fearlessly
The mist that passes like a shadow, lightly floating away
Leaving distinctions to flawed memories.

SNAKE RIVER GOAT PATHS

August 25, 1992

Narrow but well beaten paths
Weave up and down steep rock slopes.
Small beds of fine and soft dirt
Churned out at base of rock walls.
A stone bridge a foot wide
Crosses an open chasm, no bottom to see
Goat shit midway across
As if to say 'so what.'
Small cactus groves cut in half
By decades of sharp hooves.
Resting on ledge colored in lichen
Gravity pulls downward 600 feet
To a churning Snake River.

A BROOK ENTERING THE POND
July 11, 1992

Evening grosbeaks singing
High in the warmth of late afternoon pines.
The small brook weaves down into a pool.
Immersing into the cool water
The skin taught, senses contract, then expand.
Meaningless ramblings of the mind wash downstream
With the aspen leaf.
The internal clatter subsides, for in this moment
The gate swings open
The landscape now richer, whole, nuanced.

Refrain from the impulse to define, describe.
The Tao has no lexicon
The senses meld, become indistinguishable, deepen.
Navigating the undefined realms,
Senses freed of boundaries,
The mind finally calm, free
As with the brook entering the pond.

LITHIA PARK, ASHLAND

June 17, 2001

Sunrise cuts through ridge line of trees

New growth on pines burst in green illumination

Old pine bark crimson red

The park quiet in early morning

Robins and squirrels move freely between paths and brush

The benches empty

Grosbeaks ravaging seed trees

Fledgling savannah sparrows work the ground

Calls of the flycatchers roll through the thick canopy

The creek runs clear, cold

A pool beckons a wake-up plunge

Tai Chi in an amphitheater of rhododendrons

Before the paths grow busy with humans.

SAWTOOTH MOUNTAINS, IDAHO
Summer 1999

Catch a boat to cross Redfish Lake
Avoiding five miles of hiking rough terrain, talus slopes
Ascend to five thousand feet in three miles
Clouds soon build over west ridge
Temperature drops 20 degrees in 20 minutes
Push up to 8,000 feet into a corridor of granite walls
Sky turns ink black, with it the smell of heavy rain
Then thunder and hail over South Peak
A scramble into huge boulder garden
To tuck under a rock overhang
As a deafening sound of hailstones crash on granite.

Light extinguished, ground as dark as sky
No trail to be found.
Bushwhack through devils club, willow thickets, and scree
    slopes
Streams now bank-full, difficult to cross.
Reach the lake shore
No boat to cross the lake
No trail out, no moon for light
Five miles of slick rock, steep slopes, brush
The lake lost in dark

The mind dancing between anxiety and the joy of the path
    untravelled.
Arrive at cabin very late,
Spent, bloody legs, hands lacerated by rock and thorn.
Family upset, had called for a search party, now angry.
Explanations as useless as a broken compass
Only one need, finally, that seat bay the fire,
In a warm cabin.

JICARILLA APACHE LAND
July 24, 1999

Vastness understates the Northern New Mexico landscape
A protruding rock dike five feet wide, 150 feet high
Cuts the open plains across miles of sage and pine
Rough-legged hawks hold still in the updrafts
Geology defining past and present
Shaping form and function
Silence from all directions
Dynamic forces woven,
Feeding the Native soul.

GARDEN HERBS
September 9, 2004

With candlelight and pen in the Pavilion
Summer's sweet scented herbs permeate the night air
The wine draws down
The body a little older.
The moon, as with past bold silver orbs,
Paints bamboo leaves across the stone steps
While poems are written, to be re-written later.
Ink sketches of bamboo stalks will stoke next winter's fires.
Memories come and go like moths at the candle.
Thirty years of reading the Tao and no closer to finish
The heart of the Dharma, the essence of the Noble Truths,
    remains elusive.
Yet the garden herbs lived a good year
With a humble winter, a kind summer, no harvest and no
    harm.

DRINK FROM THE STREAM
September 4, 2017

I drink from this stream
To become the granite,
The lupine, mules ear and pine needles,
The ice and snow upstream.
I drink for the joy of my throat,
The nourishment of my blood.
I drink, reuniting with all living organisms
And all life past, and
For my soul and heart.
I drink to the beauty and peace of these mountains,
To be here, at home.

THUNDERSTORM

August 28, 2011

Penetrating humidity boils up the west slope of the Cascade
    Range
Clashing with the parched dry heat of the east plateau
Steel dark thunder clouds form, push skyward in columns
The ridge line cracks and booms in lightning
The bolts deep, penetrating
Fire rolls through the forest.

A wave of energy pushes into the lower plateau
Sagebrush quivers, marking electric pulses
The five senses electrified.
A nearby pine ignites
A blanket sacrificed, to smother the flame.

The ridge line fire swells further north and south
Thick grey embers hang like a veil
Turning the morning light blood-red
The west peaks grow dull in the drifting ash.

All is quiet, no birds, deer, insects to be heard, seen
As the fire tumbles down the back-side of the ridges
The once-pervasive energy suddenly begins dissipating

The extent of the burn yet to be mapped, sobering.
A breeze whispers of impermanence
In the cycle of birth, death, beauty, resilience and
    regeneration.

PILEATED AT BLUE LAKE

No calls heard for an hour
The chopping, on an old snag, continues
Sounds of a small hatchet
Back and forth, penetrating the soft wood
The pileated woodpecker, lord of these woods

His cousin, the Ivory-billed, was known as the 'God-bird'
Now extinct, never again to be heard in the SE swamps of the
    Gulf.

A half hour climb through old forest burn, a glimpse
Black bold body, high in an old Ponderosa pine
The head stunning in it's fire-red plume
Bill thick, ivory, for chopping.
A half mile away, a call
He replies, pushes off in her direction.

SMALL LAKE BY MOUNT WASHINGTON

Peaceful, isolated
Tall trees line the shore
Casting long silhouettes across the water
The lake, the air, all still.

The sun crowns the East trees
Sudden warmth, like a blanket.
In the stillness of no sound
The restless mind grows loud.

Two young mergansers
Plumage rough, discolored
Glide across the lake
Silent, as well.

Less silent is the tease of the untamed mind
Holding no purpose or agency
As it prowls the past and future
Empty and wanting.

Yet there is another chord
Through which all sound and silence may pass
And if allowed, will fill the moment
That song of the Universe

Enter the orchestra
Birds, frogs, cracking seeds
A tone quivering in its pitch
The pull into transcendence.

Set aside the relentless appetite
For that which is not here,
Or over the ridge, later, tomorrow, next week.
All that is not here, this moment, now discard.

ANGEL'S REST

Columbia River Gorge
September 11, 2012

With the sun rising over the Cascades
We push out, East, through the early morning streets of
    Portland
Coffee, chatter, bright sun in our eyes
At trailhead strap on gear, slug down water.

A brisk hike up 1,500 feet
Through old growth and drapes of canyon waterfalls
Air clear, bright, alive and permeating
We peak before noon,
Can see 60 miles of river cutting through the mountain range

Tucked in behind huge boulders,
Drink Buddhist tea, fresh from China
I marvel at this moment,
Here with my daughter
The world holding us.

ROCK AND TEA
Columbia River Gorge
December 16, 2011

The trail, carved in basalt
Narrow, steep, ascends a volcanic pillar
At times the chest pushed against the rock face
Fingers search for hand-holds

East winds howl through dwarfed firs
The view west, twenty miles of big river
To the east, a narrowing gorge
At a wide spot, the tea cup perched into a sheltered flat rock

While geese pass far below, solace as fleeting as warmth
Thoughts of life's mistakes wrench forward
A sadness captures the moment
But for a turn, to the tea, this rock and its lichen

The wind will pass, the geese will settle with the evening
All the memories, rising with little purpose, pass out to sea
Tomorrow will be what can not be known today
But this moment, in rock and tea, an enduring peace.

HIGH SIERRAS IN JUNE

June 30, 2006

Early morning sun
Tugs the night's cold from the willow grove
Grasshoppers everywhere.

Long pine needles
Brush the rough granite
As shadows.

At the top of Granite Chief, thin air and relentless wind
Yet here, rock wrens and mountain bluebirds dance through
    the rocks
The sagebrush rich in scent.

CAIRNS

June 16, 2015

Once through the narrow canyon
We always go off trail
Scramble out of the woods and shale
To broad expanses of granite that dominate the landscape.
The cairns of rock we build to mark the way to the hidden
    Pond
We rebuild each year where hawks dislodged the stone
Each cairn pointing to the next, crisscrossing ridgelines and
    creek beds.
I see your long strides navigate the granite blocks and walls
And a broad smile as that mountain confidence builds, in joy
Anticipating the rewards of stillness and solitude at the Pond.

SHRINES ON ANNAPURNA TRAIL
November 2012

Rock shrines frequent along the trail
Some barely noticed
Small, tucked into rock crevices
Stones and prayer flags placed with intention
Replaced year after year
Each time a different hand
Each it's own temple, both guardian and guarded
A prayer, a blessing, a tug on the mala
Harmonizing the thin air, honoring the steep trail,
Gifting a warm comfort
Held in the sacredness of the Himalayas.

HIMALAYAS - I
November 29, 2012

Asia, the vast and mysterious
To trek the Himalayas, the sacred
Through hidden villages, 4,000 stone-laid steps in a day
Sunrises on Annapurna and Machapuchare, 25,000-foot
    peaks
Incense at the Boudhanath Stupa, monks chanting
Namastes shared with each passing traveler, every day
Held in the strides, the breath, the nod of deep and tranquil
    eyes.

In a moon's cycle, a long return home
To what is now foreign landscapes, colors muted and bland
Back to the crunch and grind of Western life
And its relentless empty distractions
Streets and alleys littered with disappointments
Seeking a just and meaningful transition
The path to equanimity.

PART SIX

MOUNTAINS AND RIVERS

MOUNTAIN POEMS
October 4, 2014

Early fall, early morning
Sun yet to penetrate the canyon cold
The mountain quiet except for cones, tumbling through
    pines.
The trail into the upper lakes empty
Canyon-bottom aspen bright in yellow
The arcing sun soon to warm the granite walls.

Nestled against an ancient juniper, low on the ground
A thousand spiders kite over manzanita, deerbrush, sage
With small webs, long tails, highlighted by the new sun
Migrating, like others, knowing the coming snow
For how many centuries, traveling in colonies
Across mountains, in wind and silence.

Poems, scratched in thin air, on the lakeshore sand and
The gnarled bark of centuries-old pines
Ancient poems of endless journeys
There to be read and held
For a truer cadence to wander in mountain solitude
That whisper, to the open soul on a morning path.

THE REACH OF THE FIRE

Bamboo drooping over koi pond
Water gurgling through a Chinese lantern
After five hours of travel in thick harsh smoke
A million acres of Douglas fir, Ponderosa pine and oak/
    savannah forests in flames.

Crossed many rivers and creeks, this time no stopping to
    swim
Each stream harmed, challenged, an odd color
The smaller creeks dry, coated white in fire retardant
Nothing familiar, everything perturbed, taxed, in flux
Seeking, or waiting, the new realty.

Sitting with the koi
The temperature suddenly drops unnaturally, the sky cold,
    distant
A mass transformation unfolding
All life struggling, conditions void of any certainty except
    loss.

The lives this fire touched, in inherited or created realities,
Now pushed into fractured time, unfamiliar space
Lost and found, and lost, in accelerated cycles of death and
    life

With no utility in trying to discern the why, or but for
The day stolen from the learned, from what they understood
Now swirling like these koi in this small pond
Immersed in the delusion of Being.

NO TRACE

Here lies one whose name was writ in water.

– KEATS

So it is that I will pass
Sooner by a decade or two than ever considered
Terminal infliction of the body
Irreversible, the date of passage blurry, indiscernible.

No legacies to be bought or sold.

My life in the mountains held to a law, to leave no trace
Flowers, moss, lichen never to be harmed
Eluding footprints by staying on rock, no matter the size.

My passing too shall so abide.

HEADWATERS

Winds sweep high through pine and spruce
Kinglets work low through the willows
The soft gurgle of a spring weaves through root-wads and
    tree trunks
Forest floor soft, quiet at the source

This headwater will merge with three different creeks, four
    separate rivers
And together, rejoin the ocean.

How many trees, songbirds and salmon will draw life from
    these waters
Reflecting the colors of suns, moons, minerals of basalt,
    rhyolite, andesite
Carrying the knowledge of the rhizomes
Inspiring poems of steep canyons, waterfalls, valleys and
    ocean waves
Seeding the dreams and aspirations of those available to its
    essence.

SHEATHS OF BARK

September 9, 1995

Last full moon of summer
The night warm, caressing.
You gaze at the same silver orb
A thousand miles away.
Another year we remain too far distant.

So again we will trade poems
To connect our separate and wandering souls
And contemplate the years of both good and mediocre
    poems
Sometimes indistinguishable.

Scribed in sand, etched in rock, inked on sheaths of bark
At river banks and on mountain ridges
More poems given than taken
More poems imagined than written.

PART SEVEN
TRIALS

SHADOWS AND PATTERNS

The flat stone weathered,
Speckled by shadows of hanging willow.
The creek gurgles
Softening the heat with song.
The garden still
The stone wall holding heat.
Toes dangle in the passing current
A light breeze rustles the leaves.
As with the shadows dancing across the stone step
Patterns move as quickly
As the unsettled mind.

VESTIGES OF THE SOURCE

August 1, 1990

The undisciplined mind
Races like wind across the landscape
Missing the precision
The harmony of the aggregate.
Shifting light draws endless forms across the desert expanse
The nose caressed by sage and juniper
Distant sounds a whisper to the ear.
Fleeting thoughts hijack the deeper understandings
That then pass like so much dust
Yet that essence will revisit again, patiently
Seeking a more quiet and fertile soul.

PATHS OF PERIL

We sit beneath a huge canopy of old maples and cedars
The river passing quietly by our side
We drink tea and ponder the perils of the Great Journey
Reflecting on the many distractions
The side paths so enticing, but leading us nowhere
While missing the potential that resides so near
And living in the discomfort of unwarranted fear
But, alas, we smile, acknowledging how simple it is
To be in this very moment
This, that only happens once.

A HOLLOW FEELING

February 24, 1990

A long sunny day unusual for the north winter
The pagoda warm where sunlight rests
A passage from the Sutra of the Eight Realizations of the
    Great Beings

"Do not partake in actions for profit
For that will only breed greed and passion."

Sorrow follows the reflection of how few actions are free of
    greed

The long shadows of afternoon bring a chill to the spine
The birch on the west ridge shimmers in the last light of sun
Rising to find warmth, the sutra is laid at the base of the
    bronze lamp
I leave, hollowed by thoughts of all that we miss.

MEANING
December 10, 1989

Fundamental, inherent to living consciously
The quest for greater meaning, purpose
Deeper knowledge, glimpses of the miraculous
Transcending a self defined by material accumulation
Giving without reciprocity
To glimpse the Essence permeating matter and non-matter
Where there are no words, comparisons, judgment
Where light and energy exist unfettered by useless thought,
    selfish action.

LOSS

August 10, 2012

Like free falling off a steep slope
Gone with the crack of the failing rock
One reality to the next
The deeper the chasm
The greater the loss
Or gain.

AEOLIAN COLUMNS
Veterans Hospital, Portland

Aeolian pillars stand as sentinels for the suffering
Lilting songs draft up with a passing breeze
Like a thread one could follow, seeking peace.
Songs of the gods, the groans of loss.
Whispers gently placed between the columns
Of sadness, of loss, forever permeating the space
Compelling reflection on the sorrow and pain of war
Where man's failure is never so complete.

SONNET TO MY DEAD BROTHER

It's been so long
Since our last time together
The years have slipped and sped away
And you remain gone, forever.

The memories deceptively old
Images fleeting, unsteady, less certain with each year
That past, though fragmented, that we shared
Now a whisper, in want of stitching, detail.

Only you could command such a sense of humor
Immediate and cutting perceptions of any passing character
Casting an unseen light into an otherwise dull room, then
    laughter
A clarion that such a serious life warrants a jab and joke.

The years of your mystery too many
The distance between you and family too great
You kept us wondering who you really were
Or from what you endlessly ran.

You are gone
I will never again hurt with laughter, with you
Never again to sit in a car with you unmasking each passing
    person
Never again regaled by your impersonations.

Some time ago, I thought I had resigned myself to the loss
That I had properly prepared for your inevitable death
But even today the loss I find raw and hurting
So I again submit to the pain, cherish what was, and hold
    dear the loss.

DANIEL HEAGERTY

MY FATHER'S PASSING

The garden is different
The sunlight caresses the cherry blossoms more softly
The waterfall's song a deeper resonance
The shade of the cedars cooler
The scents of spring more tentative
The thrushes call too plaintive.
The garden is different
Since my father's passing.

CLOUD MOUNTAIN RETREAT

Several days in meditation
Sitting, walking, in silence.
A path weaves through old-growth forest
At a small brook, drawn to knees
Crouched over moss-covered stones
Tears roll down my cheeks
Falling to the passing water
Flooded with memories of my father
So long ago, when unable to hold me in his arms
His suffering too great
His love trapped, inaccessible
My love unfulfilled.

ONLY ONE ORGANISM

One vast organism
Comprised of trees, shrubs, rhizomes, bacteria
Lichens, animals, life
Living and functioning as one integrated system.
We may call it a forest, an ocean, a garden
Conveniently defined and categorized, in taxonomy
Fragmenting reality, hardening the delusion of duality.
Man, lost in the ever-expanding fight to prove his
    exceptionalism
Missing a most fundamental truth
That we are neither separate nor independent of this vast
    organism
A short-term player in a universe of Universes
Soon to be spun off this planet
Discarded as unnecessary detritus
A reset of this organism, back into harmony.

FOOD CAPITALISM

In farm country
Crop harvests so large
Field trucks overloaded, lumber to markets, processors
Vegetables spill over the sides
Scatter along roadside ditches.
Tomorrow, in the city, an hour away
Blanketed cold and hungry people, 500 strong
Line up in a parking lot
Wait in long lines for the one full meal of the week.

WATCHING DREAMS

I watch myself
Watch these dreams
Of life of the mind
Like colored spots
Coming and going across closed eyes
Patterns of repetition
Part past part future
Too little of right now
Dreams consuming but not providing
Relentlessly tapping the senses
Creating stories that aren't
Instilling illusions of discomfort
Ceaselessly making the dream what it is not.

GENZAEMON

January 13, 2012

An impoverished Samurai
Alone, poor, few possessions, cupboards bare
Welcomes a traveler
Caught in a snowstorm.
With no firewood remaining
He sacrifices his beloved bonsai pine
A small but elegant member of his humble garden
To fuel a fire to warm this stranger.

MOVING SAMSARA

Non-stop ruminations
Wandering the emotional and intellectual realms
Repeating, relentlessly, constructs of the grasping mind
Despite knowing their impermanence and inherent
    inaccuracy
The self-inflicting vacant ramblings
Unable to quell relentless triggers of restlessness
But the nature of mind, if allowed, will open the sky
Freeing the swoops and swirls of the swallow
Piercing that empty blue horizon
Of peace and stillness
The Nature of Mind.

PART EIGHT

TRAILS THROUGH LIFE

GARDEN ON WISTERIA STREET

I hold that view
Of a profoundly simple path
Elegant and worldly
Rich in texture, smell,
Nested in twenty shades of green.
I hold it close, though now
A thousand miles later
While looking at my bamboo
And I am allowed
To bring you back, close to my heart
Once again
Just as we did
When we embraced good-bye, earlier
At your elegant gate
There at the Garden
On Wisteria Street.

BLUE LAKE WITH ELLA

Daylight arrives with cumulus clouds of fall pushed against a
    cold blue sky
A pileated woodpecker pulls me out of the thin-walled cabin
Where we slept cold, the healer and I
She laid silently most of the night, sleep elusive
As if still on call for those she attends in their pain and
    suffering
Just before first light she finally shifts into deep breathing
I go to the lake's edge, the sun crests the east ridge,
I send her gratitude for her selfless work
And smile to see her wrapped in Indian blankets
Finally allowing herself some healing.

OCTOBER MOON

As the full moon arcs over the canyon
Its penetrating light illuminates your soft shoulder
We both stir, awake in its brightness
And make love
You lean over me, closing the curtain on the moon
In the darkness you push your warm back into my chest
I cup your breasts
We fall into deep sleep
And the moon continues its arc.

DANIEL HEAGERTY

MEDITATION POND

A plunge into the dark pool of snow-melt
Tucked against the base of a sheer rock wall
Naked, belly down on granite, recovering warmth
Winds push down steep slopes at 9,000 ft
Two hundred-fifty million-year-old rock
Holds the warmth of the sun
The granite steadfast, no wants or needs, serene
Held in the strength of it's own consciousness,
Beyond what we are able to comprehend.

BOUNDLESS MIND

Endless streams of thoughts
Relentlessly demanding unwarranted attention
Yet holding less agency than the falling aspen leaf.

A thousand thoughts
Lighter than the breast feather of a dove.

In the stillness of the mind
A continent of peace
The treasure of the Unlimited.

TRAILWORK

Load the canvas slings
Stakes, stones, wood
Picks, axes, shovels, hoes
Set out on the trail
To restore the weathered tread, the small slides
Replacing blown-out stream crossings
Align with the new contours
Clearing small spaces for sitting in contemplation
The work never finished, always understood
The purpose, to protect the soils and water
Inviting the wanderer
In peaceful labor and grand settings.

SAN MATEO

December 26, 1981

Standing in the darkness of a dark night
Eucalyptus tower overhead
We listen to the monotony of rain
While tucked under layers of low cypress boughs
Marginally shielded from the wet
Trading stories of loved ones.

We smoke cigarettes pretending they bring warmth
And drink through our father's wine
Eventually pushed indoors by the cold
With empty cups and delusional thirst.

The next morning light captures the stare of the eucalyptus
As we stumble out of the White Pavilion we call home
The trees, looming and stolid, witness our fragility
And appear to laugh at our tender eyes and parched throats.

We sheepishly pass beneath their towering form
Curious of what they might understand of last night.
We already know we will again challenge, tonight
The rain and eucalyptus, wandering conversations, and the
    inescapable empty cups.

WITH WHO
October 17, 1981

Sitting on an old log bench
Set on a grass knoll nestled in the arboretum
The fog enshrouds the night in quiet
The pure stillness infers warmth

We feel insulated, protected
Contained by this little amphitheater
The wine kindles our animated discussions
We find ourselves compelled to perform

To illustrate our thoughts on life
We spontaneously create short plays
Encouraging each other with howling laughter
Oblivious to time

The trees grow heavily shadowed
We can almost hear the fog dripping through the leaves
Our voices muffled by the thick air
Yet our laughter rolls over the slope

On the wood bench
We hold the warmth and ease that only brothers share
Reflecting with joy and gratitude
Of so many good years together.

SPRING BIRDING

1984

Campfire of juniper
Hot and pungent
We watch bird silhouettes pass before the full moon

Eyes tired from a day scanning vast marshes
The Basin and Range wet with spring runoff
Migrating birds by the thousands

Bird journals and loose sheets of poems
Scattered around our feet
We hold close to the fire for warmth

Wrapped in old blankets carried over the decades
We read the classics of Chinese landscape poetry
Laughing as only brothers are able.

LESSON OF THE TAO

August 1, 1990

With each year
Fewer on the trail practice silence
Or the honoring of lichen.
As paths steepen with time
The greater the call for understanding, acceptance
As would a knowing sage.
The many lessons of the Tao
Nested beyond what can be explained
Ripe for the learning, with each mindful step.

A TERMINAL DISEASE

July 31, 2020

Finding the undefinable, where words have no purchase
Where no demarcation exists between self, tree, soil
Or soul and ocean, life and death.

Training the mind to view death and life through a Prism
Same light, but reflecting a wide spectrum of inseparable
    colors
Swelling the realms of consciousness
Filtering and diminishing
That which lays beyond the absent mind.

Curiosity peaking
Yearning to see the unseen
Glimpses of the other side
Living in the profoundness of the Present

Stilling the fear of impermanence
Ceasing the quest for more
Nurturing that capacity for the mystical
Roam the path's effervescent silk veils
On the last leg of this life.

PATH AT DAWN

October 1, 2012

Called to a new dawn
Drawn to the porch
The view to the mountains
To wonder what the far ridge might hold, just today.
The mists form, disperse, reform over the valley below
Sensing a thousand birds in migration
Passing between here and the rising sun.

Climb through the coastal hills
Through manzanita and madrone, on to the ridgeline
To witness a burning red orb in its roll over the east horizon
Spreading the sparkle of colors across dew-dampened greens
    and reds
To lean against an old stone wall
And capture the essence of it all, in the song of the solitaire.

NINE HAND LAKE - II

August 12, 2012

The morning soft, gentle
Sunlight reaching through the pines, reflecting on the lake's
    surface
Two young mergansers bend in, skid into the water
The lake's surface announces their arrival
Sending ripples to every recess of shoreline.
They dive in silence, rise, shake their heads
As nuthatches and chickadees work overhanging limbs.
The sun pulls a slight mist from the water
To caress the attending trees
The dawn marked in harmony
The Dharma, this living painting.

BLUE LAKE
September 14, 2012

Stillness of early morning
Entire lake surface an expansive reflecting glass
Ospreys fishing the far shore, barely visible
Sun crests the east ridge
Warming cold shoulders
A dawn bath, in light and energy
Summoning that deep Awareness, fully being in the Present.

All beings that ever were
All beings that ever will be
Here, now, in this Light
This Dawn.

FAMILY HIKE
April 22, 2007

Worried about weather, as if a foreign condition
Too much anticipating the unexpected
A venture planned around risks, not adventure
Decisions random, biased
A council of parrots.

Don't travel far to the trailhead
Preparations more than warranted
Herd, protect, guard the little ones
A map, water, bug dope
But then, alas, too soon the turn to the trail back
More important than the path forward.

TODAY'S IMPERMANENCE

Leaning against an ancient redwood
The ground soft with years of fallen needles
The thrush sings her plaintiff songs
And another million forms of life
Surrounding this place in the forest
Smells, eyes, ears
Cherishing and marveling in the experience
Knowing there is more to be revealed
Just today, this the last day
To be here fully present, in this experience, in this form
For tomorrow brings but another transformation
To another state of being, of consciousness
As life, if anything, is temporary, always in transition
So lean into this redwood and hold the impermanence
And practice the art of a deep freedom.

BLISS AT THE END

September 13, 2017

The end appears to be drawing near
The cycle small in the great cosmos
Coming to close, or open
Atoms, cells, quanta to be reconfigured
Endless images of oceans, mountains
Rivers, suns and moons
The smells of memories condensing
The spirit pulled and pushed
By the fascination with the what
The fear of the how
The anxiety of the when
The bliss at the end.

APPENDIX
ADDITIONAL POEMS

A Responsibility
July 25, 1999

Push out the boundaries, they aren't there anyway
Look to the unexpected, where deeper understanding awaits
Challenge the known, rewards rest with the unknown
Create, move outside repetition, what was
Consciousness demands intention
Neither measured nor gifted
In essence, justifying existence.

This Path
September 27, 2008

This path goes
Where it goes,
Nowhere else.
The destination as ephemeral as a morning fog
The path, the gait, the texture
The awareness
Of its being, as it is
Determines the success of this journey.

Fine needles, high in the tall pines
Fall with the soft warblings of overhead vireos
Their songs of time passing.

A Stroll at the Lake
September 9, 2007

A soft breeze rustles the aspens
As stars poke through willow leaves
The creek a soft song beneath the cattails
One owl, then another
The night so dark each step uncertain
The stroll, a poem in itself.

High Mountains
September 17, 2018

In the high mountains
The air thin, penetrating, measured
Light and colors fluid in their palettes
Here, where peace and solitude rein
The mountains offering scale to depth, breadth,
	understanding
Ancient pines stand as sentinels
Granite blocks guide and reflect
The seer and the seen the same.

A Marsh
September 4, 2006

Long limbs of yellow willow
Droop to the marsh's edge
The leaves an elegant curtain
Caressed by gentle breeze

Mountain Language
September 7, 2013

Outstretched on rock
Middle of pond
The wind cascading down granite walls
Through Jeffrey pine, then aspen
To sweep across the water's surface
A language
Of the mountains
To tune the ears
Still the mind
Watch, hear, smell, be in it.

Respect for Place
September 7, 2013

We work our way up the vast granite valley
Constantly shifting routes
Boulder gardens, manzanita slopes, then sheer cliffs
In the silence of deep respect for place.

First time together in mountains
Scaling ridgelines across exposed rock
A certain familiarity, cadence, comes to us
The lead interchangeable, easy.

We stop, marvel, with humility
At the top, the secluded pond
We drink tea
Talk of consciousness
On this late day of summer.

Alpine

The pines stand tall, silent
Nuthatches swing through hanging boughs
Morning sun crests the east ridge
A golden warmth drapes the shoulders
Granite cliff, looming over the ridge-line
Red in weathered rock
Framed in the high mount

Morning Light
June 16, 2013

The morning sun highlights
The teacup you held to your lips
The damp bath towel that still holds your sweet smell
Your silver bracelet left on the bedside table.
Last night the candlelight reflecting your bright brown eyes.
Poetry books left by the bath, on the floor by the bed.
Today's light a little richer, softer
As it filters through the veil of your lingering presence.

That Red Hue

Morning sun
Piercing through billowing smoke
Of a distant forest fire
Splashing a red hue
On already red pine bark
Almost luminescent.

With You
LTK

I still dream, carrying memories
Into these woods we shared
Some thirty-six moons ago

Cold in the darkening wind
I stir for your warmth, the scent of your hair
And wonder if these trails are, actually, now steeper

The want of your outstretched hand
Your breath through that cautious smile
Your graceful movements up rocky slopes

I know the next time through here
I will again hold the space, for dreams and memories
Of your spirit and strength.Poems in Candlelight

August 14, 2016

In the candlelight
I read Wang Wei's poems
And think of you
Leaning against my chest
In candlelight
Naked in the hot bath
Lavender and mountain salts
Reading ancient poems
Of Chinese landscapes.

Fire Above Camp

Morning sun
Piercing through massive billows of smoke
A roiling forest fire
Wild, spreading and creating it's own weather
Splashing deep hues of red and crimson across the trees
On old pines clad in thick bark already red with age
The heat and wind overbearing
The light luminescent.

Cold Mist

Sheer cliffs cut and swirl the mist into mystical patterns
Some fuse into others, forming low clouds.
The granite runs gray then to steel
The mind lost in curiosity.

Heavy snows prevailed through early spring
Waterfalls at every turn
The wind grows cold, deepens
The soul beckons to sit, be still, in reverence.

Santiam River, Niagara Park
August 9, 2012

Late morning sun now reaching the river
Canyon walls clothed in fir and cedar
August flows a deep green
Breezes shift cool to warm
Rocks' cracks filled with dried moss

In Wilderness
September 21, 2020

With patience and attention
Unfolds a deep understanding
Reaching beyond words
The self, lost to the landscape
Mental constructions fade
An emptiness remains
Simple, more than enough
A clarity encompasses all that is seen, or heard
The gate of the Wilderness.

Returning

The jolt of diving into the snow-melt lake
The scent of early morning, the flowering Mule's ear
That distant drumming of the sapsucker
Elegant expressions of Wilderness
In all it's forms and sensory triggers
Presenting manifestations of the Perfect
Ripe for the humbled allowed to see, feel, hear, smell, taste
To consent to that invitation to engage
To drift with the clouds overhead
And flow with water over the granite.

Dominion Over Tomorrow / Peony Tea
September 8, 2012

We sit beneath a canopy of maple and cedar
At our side, the river, quiet
We drink peony tea.

Discussing the perils of life
The relentless distractions that devour each day.
Why so difficult, this life of ever-present shadows
And unnamed fears?

Consumed in clinging to the impermanent
Arresting the power to let go
Not able to give yesterday its deserved pass
Or cede the delusion of dominion over tomorrow.

We sit beneath a canopy of maple and cedar
At our side, the river, quiet
We drink peony tea.

Insight Meditation Center
January 20, 2013

Through this Door
The objects meld, become non-objects
The mind lays to rest, as dualism lays to rest

If even just now, in this evening
Bringing clarity to the suchness of everything
A luminous light, piercing through all perceived objects
Exposing the delusions of undiscerning thought
To rest where the soul is genuine, meant to be.

A Fine Day
July 12, 2018

Finally back in the High Sierras
Met by that special mountain summer warmth
Climbed seven hours through boulder gardens
Over ridge lines, up and down dry waterfalls

Ablutions and a swim at 8600 feet
Pureh tea under an ancient Jeffrey pine
We rested, shared thoughts of worldly attachments and
    impermanence
As yellow warblers wove through nearby willows.

Swallows danced in the blue sky overhead
A deep peace cupped and held our souls
The world of man tenuous, fleeting
What need, for anything more?
Listening as if to a soft voice
The rain rolls through the wide valley
Bringing the smell of wet soil

The Horizon Is Diminished

Offshore, large rafts of pelicans
Surrounded by rugged landscape
Stretched by late afternoon shadows
Sunset hues, a pallet of pink and red overhead
With you on the shoreline,
Even this vast landscape,
Would be diminished in your absence.

Lucidity
May 10, 2012

Ultimately
Beyond description
Beyond scrutiny
No object, form or even feeling
As if a pure silence, or
An indescribable chord
The light from non-light
Ultimately, the absolute Now
Perfectly
Lucid.